D0618252

What Is an
Artist?

To Doug and Scott—B.L.
To my family—Cliff, Andy, Jocelyn, and Lisa—C.K.

Published by The Millbrook Press, Inc.
2 Old New Milford Road
Brookfield, CT 06804
www.millbrookpress.com

Library of Congress Cataloging-in-Publication Data
Lehn, Barbara.
What is an artist? / Barbara Lehn ; photographs by Carol Krauss.
p. cm.
Summary: Simple text and photographs depict young people engaged in
activities that embody the qualities of an artist.
ISBN 0-7613-2259-0
1. Artists—Pictorial works—Juvenile literature. 2. Art—Vocational
guidance—Juvenile literature. [1. Artists. 2. Occupations.] I. Krauss,
Carol, ill. II. Title.
N8350 .L44 2002
709'.22'2—dc21
2001007864

Special thanks to all the children, families, and organizations
who contributed to this book, especially Emerson Umbrella Center
for the Arts, Concord, Massachusetts.

What Is an Artist?

Barbara Lehn

Photographs by Carol Krauss

The Millbrook Press
Brookfield, Connecticut

An artist is someone who **expresses** an **idea** that someone else can see.

William paints a picture of an astronaut traveling in space.

"These are microphones on his helmet because I think he needs to talk," says William.

An artist **shares feelings** through art.

Henry illustrates a story about a misunderstanding he had with his twin sister, Kate.

"When I asked if she was still mad, Kate thought I said she smelled bad. I'm going to show the frustration in my face by making my eyebrows squeeze together," explains Henry.

An artist learns about materials.

Max is learning how to handle clay on a pottery wheel.

Sarah guides Max, "Push gently against the sides like this so the pot doesn't collapse."

An artist learns how to control **composition**.

Currin designs a border for her collage.

"I'm going to put yellow strips of paper around the sides so the center will stand out," plans Currin.

An artist **practices** skills.

Nikki shows Amanda how she got less paint on the paper.

"I push the brush against the side of the cup and I can paint without dripping," Nikki explains.

An artist is a **problem solver**.

Jazzy, Emma, and their friends are putting the finishing touches on a boat they made.

"We need to add more tape to the rudder and the mast, or it will fall apart when we take it outside," Jazzy and Emma decide.

An artist gets inspiration from **nature**.

Matt is drawing a view of the ocean.

"I'm going to smudge the blue into the purple to make it the same as the color I see," says Matt.

An artist learns to use **new tools** to make art.

Cate drew a picture of her cat and scanned it into her computer.

"A colored background makes my cat look better," Cate thinks.

An artist gets **inspiration** and support from others.

Luke enjoys painting in his dad's art studio.

"How can I show the fireman inside the truck, Dad?" asks Luke.

An artist is open to the **unexpected**.

Alice is trying to make a pinkish shade of red.

"This isn't the color I had in mind, but I like this color better!" discovers Alice.

An artist exercises her imagination.

Katherine carefully attaches loops to her sculpture.

"This is what I thought of when I saw my lump of clay," Katherine tells Shannon.

An artist knows that making **mistakes** is part of the process.

Hannah changes the birds in her picture.

"These wings are uneven, so I'm going to make one side fatter," says Hannah.

An artist has **fun**!

Kippy, Sam, Chris, and Brittany are paint-fencing.

Chris shouts, "We got more paint and we'll rescue you, Kippy!"

An artist is a person who . . .

expresses ideas

expresses feelings

learns about
materials

controls
composition

practices skills

is a problem solver

studies nature

learns to use
new tools

gets inspired by others

learns from
mistakes

imagines

discovers the
unexpected

has fun!

That's
what an
artist
is!

About the **Author** and **Photographer**

Barbara Lehn has been involved in regular and special education for more than 25 years. She currently teaches first grade in Concord, Massachusetts, where she continually learns from her students. Barbara lives in Andover, Massachusetts, with her husband and their son.

Carol Krauss turned to professional photography after a career in management consulting. Her black and white fine art prints can be seen at a variety of New England galleries. She also does freelance photography for individuals and businesses in the area. She has collaborated with her friend Barbara Lehn on two other books—WHAT IS A SCIENTIST?, and WHAT IS A TEACHER? Carol live in Concord, Massachusetts with her family and dog.